The Czar

The Czar

Mary Biddinger & Jay Robinson

Black
Lawrence
Press

Black
Lawrence
Press

www.blacklawrence.com

Executive Editor: Diane Goettel
Book and cover design: Amy Freels
Cover art: "Mark Twain Motel" by Jay Robinson

Copyright © 2016 Mary Biddinger & Jay Robinson
ISBN: 978-1-62557-948-5

Published 2016 by Black Lawrence Press.
Printed in the United States.

For all the Czars.

Contents

III. The Czar

"I am not yet ready to be Tsar. I know nothing of the business of ruling."
—Nicholas II

I. The Czar

THE CZAR

Somebody called it a bestiary
but it was best when on its knees

as if each of the beasts
were kites and I was young again,

without sin. Let's move,
you said, but to a place without

hills. Empire-building isn't
a facile task. All that red velvet

like blood pools on floor
tiles, like the afternoon we once

spent in a deer stand. Bottle
caps for necklaces, an incomplete

deck of cards. You told me
you invented the playoff beard.

I said your thighs resembled
a cruise ship inching

toward the shore, but it was
still too frigid to rip off

your coveralls. Breath in the air
like fingerprints. Is it true

there's a castle inside your castle,
rescue birds guarding the moat?

Let me play the princess
again and you can be the horse

I rode in on. They say you know
what happens when the lights

go out. All of this, I explained, feels
like it's happening in a secret

location. And a week later
your thighs winked at me. Someone

on the television declared, Well,
they're not making any more

beachfront property. I wasn't
a docile servant any longer.

THE CZAR

To those who can afford underpinnings of quality.

To those who dine on other people's roof-straw.

To those directly responsible for increased surveillance.

To those owls who know but don't consent or tell.

To those whose voting stickers never adhere.

To those princes you dealt with accordingly.

To those who doubt the true innuendos of torture.

To those directly responsible for Miley Cyrus.

To those pollsters you later seduced with mints.

To those who insist every vote should count twice.

To those who dine on salami every day for lunch.

To those faxes we sullied with biological materials.

To those who grow a beard when they shouldn't.

To those undergraduates who dine on each other.

To those walls you climbed—naked and drunk on icing.

To those who secured the borders of my pants.

To those workers who bodyguard the potholes.

To those who cannot afford free health care.

To those directly responsible for bathing the Czar.

To those directly responsible for the Virgin Afterbirth.

To those peaches, actual peaches, not innuendos.

To those miniskirts I refused to wear in the elevator.

To those owls who occupied Wall Street.

To those directly responsible for your orgasm.

THE CZAR

The Czar does not feel
like ruling today. He says
a mistress is just another

hole in the bowling ball.
Bed sheets like permanent
records. In the morning

the three of us share iced
black coffee from a to-go cup.
He doesn't smile as we fight

over his straw. The TV
blasting to drown out
the sounds of an entire

empire crying. Sometimes,
he says, the teleprompter
makes important choices:

what costumes to wear
to the masquerade, or even
which province to invade,

the princess impregnated
with various indignities.
Like the Vienna sausages

wedged in their sad casings
at the Super Bowl party.
When we go to bed

each night, he tells us
it's going to be The Game
of the Century. The two

of us appreciate how
the Czar believes violence
to be a stringed instrument.

Sometimes he's a baby
in his imperial mildness,
the way Louis XIV bathed

in the light of a hundred
backlit keypads, all the pins
laying down before his strike.

THE CZAR

has a sister. This much is true.
Every girl in this kingdom
and the next wishes it were

her glass slippers in his hands.
Including myself. Who am I
kidding? There is no other

kingdom. All of us have
memorized the fine features
of the Grand Duchess, her cruel

bangs, dark eye shadow, like
verses from the bibles we torched
and outlawed so long ago. Later,

the Czar fed the ashes to the poor.
Of course, the Grand Duchess
has yet to make her societal

debut. For years we have only
followed her on Instagram.
The rumors about the rumors

about her persist. This much
is also true. Perhaps she's just
a character in an old ditty:

you know, the gal you'd slide
across your knee and paddle.
One neighborhood can't hold

this much vaudeville, so it spills
into the county, like a detergent
floe, or the naughty sister come

home from a terrible date, no
measure of Dreft enough to tidy
all that human sweat from one eye.

THE CZAR

When I paint my monarch in watercolor
I half expect him to sentence me

to twenty years hard labor. My biscuits
unphenomenal. All the Alexandrines

in my notebook unremarkable.
Just another girl with coal hair, ready

to boil a pot of beets, leaves, and ashes.
My monarch and I never completed

each other's exercise programs.
No attempt to traverse the passageway

of intrusion. So many stoplights
in his kingdom, and he as colorblind

as a prairie dog. Nightly when I hem
my monarch's garments, I am mending

the chiffon of my own discontent.
He will never read this. His version

of literacy involves a military campaign
against the gorillas at the zoo.

Confession: I do not write Alexandrines.
My notebook not a notebook. Confession:

I have been plotting my own illicit
self-portrait for years. The photographs

I've taken in black and white lack
recognition. Confession: recognition

has never been my aperture. Sentence
me, my Lord. Tie me to an outpost.

THE CZAR

The Czar declares it is too early
to be speaking German. He declares
this in German. He ransacks

his study for an illuminated
manuscript on the tenuous nature
of our attachments. One day

you're sitting in a dull literary
theory class, the next touching
the man across the room from you

in a dull literary theory class,
and no dull literary theory has ever
ventured to explain this. Maybe

he'll become your new Czar, or
at least the Czar of the week. You
voted against the partial-Czar-

abortion bill, but then took hard
showers in the town plaza and ate
the berries from questionable

bushes. You lecture your own
literary theory students on nothing
but *Das Unheimliche*, because who

needs the same thing twice. Unless
the same thing isn't the Czar
and rejects the Czar, his affinity

for corks from the finest wines
possible at the Circle K. Something
Derrida would never deconstruct.

Something never so dull as
the feel of the non-Czar's fingers
on your latest manuscript.

THE CZAR

Sometimes I imagine the Czar as the Czar
of another kingdom, or a sorority.
The latticework on the castle walls

white and climbable. The latest rumors
say his throne isn't a throne at all.
At the parade, we ate sausage rolls, truffles,

deflated the tires of the senator's float.
We were never even taken into custody.
The next afternoon you couldn't be trusted

to babysit the ancient Crock-Pot or dress
the one deer we'd always been meant
to devour. You said, My name is the Czar

and I approve this message. I kept my
apron strings tied. Clogs on my feet.
All the bees at the window, looking

to sting something. The problem was
you were the Czar, esteemed vice
provost of Czar State University, or

chancellor of Czar Technical College,
home of the Fighting Screws. Apparently
my destiny was to become *just another*

plaything. I had taken part in an ancient
tradition, like the way you fetished
miniatures of your own countenance

despite the taboo. Sometimes I imagine
the Czar's visage superimposed on my
pantalets. Oh, the ballads he sings there!

THE CZAR

is just one of many big-ticket purchases,
but eventually the Czar, too, will seize up

during a load of whites, or defrost a shelf
lined with that nasty brick of wedding cake

his mother insisted you keep and eat one
year later. There's no interest-free credit

on a Czar, and you can see why. The lack
of return policy is self-explanatory.

He loves his couch and his dogs. He loves
dirty snow and sagging rooftops, dull

statuary of children throwing stones
or rotten pineapples at a passing beggar.

There are no Czar photo albums or tea
cozies with the likeness of the Czar

embroidered in junior bear suit, no
junior panic attacks or muffled orgasms

in the Kingdom of Czar. The fine print
of the Czar reads like the soft lyrics

of a Brazilian songstress. Really, the Czar
only wants to show his money maker

to the general public. He has a tight grip
on the proverbial steering column.

They say he refuses to rule in proverbs
or aphorisms. But they don't know his

attempt to override the stale economic
discourse with a high-end pony detector.

THE CZAR

is a little worried about how much he loves the novel *Wuthering Heights*. In private, he whispers, "I am _____" then sends himself to un-Heaven. Who is the naughtier child, Catherine or Heathcliff? And why doesn't the weather in Czarland Heights vacillate like a northern place with moors and hillocks? He can't say that Heaven wouldn't want him, as he invented the concept. Why did it have to involve heaps of coconut? Why was his movie in black and white, and replete with ringlets, the dogs dead for decades? In a less probable world, the Czar would have also been a Czar. Yes. In a less probable world, though, Edgar wouldn't have died. And the peasants would have feasted nightly on more than limburger cheese and half-stale crackers. Before the Brontë sisters, he considered books an accelerant. Like his mistress's faux bridal lace teddy. Or the Lady Czar's culinary renderings of aimless heft. At night he stares out the castle windows. A low, accusatory moon in the Czar-like sky. Stray cats in an alley and a pail of warm milk. Low water level in the moat. He sips Glenfiddich by the gallon, tells his mistress he will stay up all night until he finds the right word. But he never does.

THE CZAR

The Czar's impotency is all over
the news. It took me a minute
to recognize the headlines

as commentary on foreign policy
resolutions. There is no polite way
to say these things or otherwise

investigate the Czar like some kind
of flannel pajama detective. Do
you recall the intense uncertainty

of our standing in the kingdom?
His mistress couldn't recall
anything before her third glass

of scotch. I laced each one
with religious ecstasy, the notes
from the scene of the crime.

The Czar remained unaware
of our conversations. I reversed
the switch from Tide to Wisk,

and he called it a conversion. His
mistress overthrown. She insists
on alternative methods for

intimate cleansing. Thinks the icing
on every cake is just edible
laces on a cut-rate bustier. *Back*

then, the Czar quips, *the girls
could stand erect on their own.*
He tries the black coffee method

but the results are too anxious.
Instead, he waxes the moustache
of yet another banana republic.

THE CZAR

Let the record show the leaves fall only for the Czar.

Let the record show I sold his story to *The Enquirer*.

Let the record show I'm not wearing pajama pants.

Let the record show my descent was inevitable.

Let the record show the Czar's mistress speaks in tongues.

Let the record show how I spied on the NSA.

Let the record show the warrants have been exercised.

Let the record show 7 minutes is certainly enough.

Let the record show I misspelled *aphrodisiac*.

Let the record show the Czar's typos preserved in stone.

Let the record show I skipped the 10-step program.

Let the record show my Czar-shaped birthmark.

Let the record show the rebar underneath the bridge.

Let the record show the clocks never turned back.

Let the record show that length is always an estimate.

Let the record show that there's always some slippage.

THE CZAR

Ironically, the Czar was a terrible student of foreign languages. His parents complained to the principal. He called his *OEUVRE* his *OUVRIR*. He'd spend the rest of his life attempting *to open* someone or another. The Czar thought a body of work was *for sex* (emphasis mine). His biggest challenge was the pluperfect. One day he was taking a piss at work and terrified himself with the prospect of pissing in the same pissoire for the next thirty years. Not to mention...

The Czar recalled the word for rabbit in French, but asked for a fish at the small game restaurant. We will not speak of the brief tutorial regarding Belgian engineering. In Mexico, the Czar announced himself as an organ thief, and then placed his request for The Entertainer. He claimed *Sister Carrie* to be his favorite Russian novel, the best cure for hangover to be another trip to Las Vegas. What happens in the Czar's fancy room never stays in the Czar's fancy room...

Once, as a sophomore in college, the Czar drove to Canada. He took a wrong turn, ended up in Montreal instead of Windsor. Every map looks like it's written in the Cyrillic alphabet, he said to his roommate. But he had a bottle of Wild Irish Rose in a thermos and one foot out the window. Both of them drunk on freedom for the better part of a dozen hours. The Czar thought the Cyrillic alphabet a soup he hadn't been served as a boy. His roommate laughed, got left beside a sagging barn outside Ottawa...

But the Czar can roll a joint in any language. As a Czar, he could make a priest confess. We will not speak of this, the Czar mumbles to an otherwise preoccupied prostitute in German. We will not speak of this...

THE CZAR

Can you keep a secret? The Czar
gave me an Advent calendar as a gift.

Have you ever felt real ermine
at the bottom of a damp steel box?

Neither have I. A storm blasts
even the strongest poplars into sheep.

I've spent too much time trying to
find the missing half of my figurative

locket. Do you know how to use
a genuine knife, or would you like this

imitation? Don't ask why rocks
are slippery. Sometimes the only thing

I have left is my religion. I open
the first box. Inside is a tiny note

that says, This is my gift to you.
Needless to say, I hoped for more.

Sometimes the gifts we give are
bound by the trade deficit. The Czar

and I at first traded exclusively
in glances at his mistress. Both of us

wanted her underneath the tree
at the center of the city, although

for different purposes. These things
my therapist says not to discuss.

Once again, I have had too much
sangria. The debt ceiling is spinning.

The Czar's campaign motto promised
he would hold back my hair.

THE CZAR

loves the Lady Czar, but she is no Czarina,
if you catch my drift. In a rudimentary

assessment of women, the Czar seems
to have reeled in a fish too big for his net.

They met when she was hostessing
a discount seafood emporium in Maine.

No, they met in the wide maw of a whale
in January, this being the only shelter,

all the raves shuttered in the offseason.
The Czar boasted a Mental Age of ten,

and his heart was the size of a stapler.
Behold my assets, glowered the Czar,

and yet nobody told him his political
cartoon likeness was a work of realism.

The Lady Czar loves Hummels but not
lederhosen. She bakes cakes in the exact

shape of Valentine hearts. She refuses
the lessons a corset can teach you.

In other words she's no foreign Czarina.
The Czar finds himself so often trapped

within the renovated apocalypse bunker.
An exchange of various peace offerings,

the Czar speaking in German again, his
bald intentions backlit by a Bunsen burner.

THE CZAR

Every morning I wake: the taste
of blood in my mouth. I'd call

it metallic, but I haven't eaten
for months. The coins I swallowed

disappeared. There is a rumor
that our borders are expanding.

Like the universe. But it's hard to see
past the tea lights in the garden.

I want to press a button, make
cappuccino appear. The foam

on my mouth actual foam. Not
the chloroform of my youth. Czar,

they say you aren't a constellation.
In other words, heavenly. Clearly

they haven't seen your back or
your profile in shadow. Insomnia

has stopped by again. Like an
infomercial. In our Constitution

our inalienable rights aren't even
mentioned or ignored. In our

Constitution the destitute
are simply a footnote. Who makes

homespun documents, anyway?
It's impossible to discern which

candle is *caramel latte* and which is
shoulder on a sultry day. Every

morning I crush out the stub
of improper longings. Dirty work.

Give me something to venerate,
and make it impossibly fast.

THE CZAR

The Czar's revolution revised the hem of my nightgown.

The Czar's revolution was most certainly televised.

The Czar's revolution involved a suite at the Ritz.

The Czar's revolution irrevocably altered the breakfast menu.

The Czar's revolution mandated yoga pants for everyone.

The Czar's revolution opened the gates of my thighs.

The Czar's revolution not nearly as pornographic as I hoped.

The Czar's revolution was our best kept secret.

The Czar's revolution irrevocably altered my best dress.

The Czar's revolution outlawed my Bill of Rights.

The Czar's revolution mandated severe neglect.

The Czar's revolution defined the scope of my serfdom.

The Czar's revolution included room service.

The Czar's revolution was a hoax, according to the tabloids.

The Czar's revolution did more than burn a little.

The Czar's revolution was not an anti-flea medication for cats.

The Czar's revolution unspun most of the vinyl.

The Czar's revolution had nothing to do with the sun.

The Czar's revolution: you did not say you wanted it.

THE CZAR

is in love with his older sister. This is a problem. The Czar for years aware of the ever-widening difficulty of finding her in exile. Probably on an island surrounded by witches in leather skirts. Or somewhere in America, wasted on Schlitz, and always on the Twitter. Where did his father banish revolutionaries and their theses, the milk maids he'd seduced, whose mouths he tired of in less than two minutes? The apple never falls far from the tree. But, in this case, we're talking about two different trees fighting over the same apple, even though one tree was slain by the other. Incest is the least of the problems in a place like this, the Czar's mistress says. And she flips back the channel to watch the final segment of another episode of *House Hunters International*. Tonight: her hair in pigtails, like the daguerreotype of his 13-year-old great-grandmother on the mantle. His sister an exact replica in the one charcoal drawing of her that survived the purge. The page stained with organic tea, a speck of a cherry sucker caked to one corner. Like the original cover of *Flowers in the Attic*, suggesting nothing of what trembled inside. Once, in Tulsa, a redheaded man leaned out of a pickup and called the Czar "a real Peter Quint, a real Nanny Hawkins." Or something similar. The Czar fears his sister is working as a domestic in a deserted castle. The Czar is unaware of literary tropes. He has no foil but his sister, who once frocked herself up in a makeshift lamé, and couldn't decide whether to love it or list it.

THE CZAR

This much is true: Abraham Lincoln
isn't coming back. On pace

for a record year, we broke even
the tenderest figurines.

Of course the Czar never leaves.
It's just a costume. Mask

of an olive branch bearer, bustle
for some restoration clown.

I once saw him bottom up near
the statue garden, hard

rain as clever aphrodisiac. Sunup
in a leaky boat, sunny side

down in the mouth of a piano forte.
Back then, we really knew

to read music like the language
of each other's skin. Lately

the tide pulls us from the shore.
My plunging neckline dips

dangerously in the water. Why
sink a coin in the fountain? Dollars

have just as much luck. I carved
our names into a cherry tree.

But not our real names. Some
servant has stolen our identities,

used them for firewood. We burn
all night. Two fires. Smoke signals

twisting in the air like the cursive
my children will never learn.

Two fires. Two burning bushes.
One on each side of The River Czar.

THE CZAR

The games the Czar played
as a child aren't so different
than the games we all played:

King of the Hill and Capture
the Milk Maid's Virtue.
Only the consequences

differ, signal with a wink
to the firing squad to aim
a BB gun with great

intent. Of course, the Czar
still plays these games
and otherwise hangs your

underwear on the branches
of various government
programs. The Czar's version

of universal health care
suffers under the weight
of preexisting conditions.

He buys his little blue pills
at six bucks apiece, refuses
any friendly discount offered

by suspicious websites. He
considers himself a Free Trial
with no strings attached.

Unless you count the strings
of an apron tied around
somebody's flaccid retainer.

The Czar can't bob for apples
or sketch a sustainable
hangman. He blames these

shortcomings on his many
war wounds: kamikaze
madrigal feast, flaming

Swan Lake, the boy's
choir populated by mini
aspirational Czars in green

satin cummerbunds. How
many cummerbunds has our
fair Czar worn in his day?

To speak plainly, the world
is his cummerbund. Eternal
ring of joy around the Czar.

THE CZAR

The Czar called me an emotional double agent.
I mean, who isn't? Mama always hides

the cookies on the top shelf, if you know what
I mean. Here with my Czar, I feel

safest of all. The bird of prey sanctuary mostly
holds paper cups with tears

in the bottom. I feel for them. I only had White
Hen sandwiches and thin gravy.

I only had a lot of things I didn't have. Like
my best disguise. The Czar set

goals for my activities. He put me in charge
of his talking points. He told me,

You should feel as comfortable as a small boy
on a trip to the library. He didn't say

how many books on disabled dogs to check out.
Or whether I should also let the wolf

or the bear guard the bathtub. I chose both.
I became domesticated.

He said, I told you you were emotional. Difficult
to tell the tone of irony when

you've snagged your fishnets on a sheepskin
rug. He covered my breasts

with his generous hands. He took one look
at my stockings and said

he wanted to discuss my wardrobe with me.
But I wasn't wearing anything else.

THE CZAR

declares a pox on all non-British literature. He's named his mistress *Pride* and Lady Czar *Prejudice*. I call them Bangers and Mash instead. The SparkNotes version omits the afternoon bliss of two women in two separate great rooms sticking a singular doll in the Czar's likeness with rusty pins.

The Czar has funded a committee of scientists tasked with the resurrection of the Brontë sisters. He says he wants Emily cast as The Girl with the Dragon Tattoo. But he also prefers their masculine pseudonyms. A little gender confusion, his mistress confessed on the night she Joan of Arc'd her hair, is good for the soul. Like chicken salad. Or baby oil stained sheets.

The Czar relocates his birthday on the calendar to coincide with Anne's. Agnes Gray, he likes to say, should have been my governess. The Czar is having a difficult time distinguishing fact from fiction again. It's genetic, according to his mother. She said she was a Charlotte, but she wanted to be a Samantha. She wanted to develop a sympathetic sinus disorder. I mean, who doesn't?

The Czar claims to have an internal decoder ring. It's like that spaghetti in a shoebox trick. Decades ago, the Czar's mother bundled him with his sister and a raging case of pox, woolen underwear flung over the radiator. It was the contagion game, he later learned, and even the storybooks itched. All the bonnets had a disproportionate number of bees. Please do not ask about scarring or organ damage. One can never be too close to a sister.

THE CZAR

Sometimes the czar is no czar.
This happens infrequently.
On Halloween he dresses

in his best Czar costume, as if
pinstripes were a voter
mandate. But what is a Czar

really, his mistress likes to say,
into the boudoir mirror.
Once again, she's misplaced

a pearl necklace. Once again,
she's a soiled boutonniere,
a shattered candy cane.

The Czar unbuttons another
button in reply. It's difficult
to share both a Czar and

a dressing room. Sometimes
the Czar is both a Czar and
a Madrigal, his mistress

on a street corner or crowded
square filling a wine-stained
Styrofoam cup with offensive

notes. It all started urgent,
with pleas for bus change,
then transformed into attic

rooms and breathlessness,
a sense of having been there
previously. When the Czar

is no Czar, he is the beggar
Czar. He does not need to
sleep on his boots or itch

his own boils. In any realm,
the Czar has staff. Who needs
a globe when the world feels

you back? This is my costume,
the Czar declares to the night-
club door. And yes, it was.

THE CZAR

has nicknamed himself Frankie
Machine. He has heavily annotated

my copy of *The Man with the Golden
Arm*. What an asshole! Lou Reed

is dead at 71. Why go on? Everyone is
riddled with shrapnel from war.

You know the type: hop a wrong train
and next thing you're a novel

away from a spry Italian bookie and
a woman lighter than her own

shawl. Sometimes I think my sexuality
would make a great libretto

for street opera. Enter Czar, literally
dripping with potential. He

can wear harem pants into the twenty-
first century. The woodwinds

start up like a stampede of ants
at a picnic we didn't plan on because

we wanted to eat lunch. The Czar
then holds a press conference

in his bedroom. Only he was the one
asking questions. Slowly, I

dissected his rhetorical strategy.
Pathos is a character I'd undress,

I said, as if the kingdom were a novel
and I couldn't hear the flute solo.

THE CZAR

Today is National Czar Day,
but so is every other day. Like

a cloud of blackbirds. It's
really just another afternoon

of clean fetishes and excuses
to stuff into your best Czar

face a third slice of Aunt
Desdemona's so-called

Sugar Tits Cake. The Czar's
image composed solely

of user-generated content,
all-too-filled desires, and

other sacraments. Ha ha.
Like bathing in the societal

birdbath or asking for
another nipple to be dipped

into the fountain. It's not
always clear when the Czar's

innuendos are innuendos
and when they're really

a second helping of the main
course, or what he calls

economic discourse. In
other words, today precludes

the permissibility of anything
except moderation.

The Czar watches a hole fill
with rainwater. Ha ha.

The Czar once worked
in a barren office

for a woman named Mecca.
Ha ha. The Czar type

swerves crazy into oncoming
lanes to skip chuckholes

or lost blonde hairpieces.
He's no chemist—those

white lab coats demeaning—
but he is all shelf life.

II. The Revolution

THE REVOLUTION

The Czar's beard looks a little too long today.

Like he invented the word *mesmeric*, or squints

in the mirror and sees himself as just a speck

of sea salt on the caramel holiday popcorn.

At night, he closes the chamber doors, lights

a roaring fire, sits at his desk, as if it's a throne

and he's not drafting what he calls *The Revolution*:

A Working Title. He means this both as irony

and metanarrative, but doesn't have a clear

definition of either. Someday he'll be the essence

of things non-Czar, cold as a salmon swimming

against the current of Lady Czar's thighs. A boy

has earned the title of Czar at the Goth club,

Detroit circa 1997, and he's in clothes owned

by his countrypeople, right down to the chain-

mail and claustrophobic boots. He's wearing

a fragrance called RAIN, but more like leather

on leather on leather on yes on leather on yes.

The Czar understands how beard length can

affect overall viability and verisimilitude.

And he defers. Beyond the beard in the mirror

The Czar can barely float. The teen moms

and homemade porn. Lady Gaga dressed up

as a tax return. If a tree falls in the woods

there's going to be an investigation, a press

tour, and a tell-all biography of his testicles.

. . . .

Is any of this preferable? his mistress asks.

She's reviewing color samples for edible lace

teddies. She's started her own line. Who hasn't?

The next Czar huffs paints in the basement

of the book repository, alters the spelling

of *Czar* to *Csar*, marries his second and third

cousin, a pair of matryoshka dolls he keeps

under his hoodie. Hyperbolized rage, leather

chaps, Nintendinitis. The kingdom, Lady Czar

laments, for which there is no inoculation.

But not everybody can manage an inbox

like Lady Czar. No spam eludes her.

She notes that every hook in the house looks

either phallic or hyper-phallic, and then

nothing cannot arouse her, then nothing can.

Why do we always secretly hope

for a natural disaster, if only for the chance

to cling to another man's life dinghy

instead of our own? Survival instinct, of course.

True desperate days of the revolution,

the kind where ladies befriend even the pill

bugs in their cell corners, pen memoirs

on upturned palms. We all hope for a cell

that's a double-chamber, meaning cold

incarceration with one's naughty self,

the good self making all kinds of awful deals

with authorities, accepting a pair of hot

mittens, soap fragments, promise of fresh

login information. The bad self looms something

like a gargoyle, like the guy in math class

who kept singing "Hush" by Deep Purple then

denying it, while your good self complained

and your bad self fantasized about how to

stop the music, so to speak. Not everybody

can be both *protagonist* and *creep on a precipice*

in a thinly-veiled Roman de Clef starring

former child prodigies and owners of prodigious

racks. I'm always cold. I waste abundant time

thinking about the notion of a Lingua Franca,

and the rate for a mustache ride no longer

meets the Gold Standard, despite inflation.

. . . .

These days you put a little bit of this, then

      a little bit of that into the pan, but still

the cake emerges from the oven transformed

      into a pile of receipts. Baking is not the same

as cooking. Cooking is tangible, like a tornado

      warning. Or Lady Czar uncorking another

peach wine cooler in the servant's chambers.

      Even the dog hears it. And the Czar prank

calls not only strangers, but people he knows.

      Check out my legerdemain, he whispers into

the hot receiver. Only his voice is cracking, so

      the librarian just hears a queer toaster-rattle.

When people suggest you put that in your pipe

      and smoke it, do they really know how long

it is? I'm just messing with you. In Chapter IV

      there may or may not be a blatant allusion to

an underground club selling raw milk, verboten

shaving cream. On his weekly radio address

the Czar issues edicts on bloated ankles, outlaws

all public displays of his erection. In other

words, he's finally let the owl out of the bag,

Lady Czar says and nods to the mistress.

Sometimes, the Czar thinks, The Revolution

will never end because he isn't sure if

it ever began, or when or where or whether

he still has the right knee-high football

socks for an execution. People bang fists

on the castle door, then Tweet accordingly.

As if The Revolution were a hashtag and not

what you and your neighbor's sister attempted

behind closed doors because you read about it

in a book once, and called it Experimentation.

III. The Czar

THE CZAR

has allowed his visage to appear on a placemat.
It's not New York, but at least it's not Sacramento,

either. The Czar hates the film *Lost in Translation*.
He thinks it has no action. What a dolt, this Czar,

who bides his time in a room listening to the coo
of a hair dryer, who hires a maid to pluck hairs

from his horsehair furniture. They say the owl
was a Czar's daughter, but the branches stood too

erect for her liking, and now she's a public house.
She's a donkey bray, a wayward military complex.

Back in the day, there were homes for Czars who
got themselves in a little trouble. Heavy curtains.

Rocking chairs fused to the floors. Ponderous
awnings and constant flow of assault missiles.

Every football stadium in Czarland is named
after the Czar, and his team adrift, winless.

Lady Czar doesn't even know football exists.
She's all cattle and no hat, his mistress says. But

it's been a long time since the Czar had to spend
any time in a barn or reevaluate his plans

to cultivate a genetic likeness. When the Czar
speaks, is anyone really listening? The Czar

Theorem couldn't secure funding to research
anything more than finding a cure for democracy.

The Czar sighs. All day long the Czar sighs. But
he's a wide omnipotent grin on those placemats.

THE CZAR

It's true the Czar was kidnapped
as a child. All the earmarkings
of the Lindbergh baby, and more.

Somebody left the windows
open. Somebody else flipped
on the lights. Then the Supreme

Investigator found the Czar
in the nick of time underneath
the stairs quoting the script

to the series finale of *The Sopranos*.
Does anything glow in the dark
anymore? Like the scorched earth

or pine needles yellowed with piss.
I've heard the Czar still toys
with the reactors in the dollhouse

his sister built for me. Walls
papered with parakeet feathers.
The smallest pearl ever discovered

for a doorknob. Sometimes
he takes the baby we made and
covers it with fur and hides it

in a secret passageway. Even
non-tabloids thought it so peculiar
that plain, non-violent non-women

empathized with a rageful figure
who had corpulent tendencies, vast
depression, extensive underworld

connections. But the Czar was built
for the masses. Of course ducks
fly away, leaving us in a diner booth,

victims of our own elastic, wishing
a stranger with a burlap sack
would shut the lights off for good.

THE CZAR

is a frequent motif in contemporary literature.

is a list of mild complaints, such as hangnails, only human.

is my childhood trip to the forest, my fear of axes.

is a buck who dares to wander a playground in November.

is foil to lesser characters who serve to highlight his grandeur.

is just a delusion, really.

is a fancy name for chemical imbalance, fear of ladders.

is why men pretend they did not grow up in backwoods places.

is the top of a sledding hill, but never the bottom.

is why I do all these things, try to create a sense of history.

is all I see in my child's maple leaf impersonation.

is a charade, or at least the thought of a charade.

is a simile, not a metaphor.

is a song played on repeat and shuffle at the same time.

is a medication we're all taking orally.

is a diagnosis, not a prescription, a note left on bathroom mirror.

is my childhood fascination with the smell of gasoline.

is a femme fatale in drag once the lights go out.

is a scab I keep picking, a sad boot tied to a tree branch.

is the difference between an obsession and a compulsion.

is not limited by pages numbers or marginalia.

is everyone's juvenilia in Czar form.

is his own font.

is an autopsy, not a diagnosis.

THE CZAR

endeavors to become proficient in Art History. Step one: shutter the wine bar and dump all pastries resembling breasts. Step two: drape shawls over any paintings that depict the human body in agony and/or ecstasy. What's left: photographs of indifferent snails, a pretentious collection of beer steins.

endeavors to become "a better dresser, a real bon vivant." Supply list: Petroleum jelly. Pinstripes. Comb + waxed paper. Scrapbook from Madonna's Blonde Ambition tour. Savoir faire. Extensions. Retractors. Spray starch. Eggplant cutlets sprinkled with salt. One tall bottle of Mane & Tail. Bleach.

endeavors to write the novel that has always been inside him, like a bad meal. He gathers his finest clichés, buys a book for free on his phone. The writing is tiny as grains of amaranth, but many thoughts are small before properly stoked. Many books start out as nightmares that end in sick.

endeavors to hold onto his mistress a little longer. Like she's a cassette from his collection of mix tapes. Not the handcuffs under the mattress, the key between his teeth. Step one: have her arrested on charges of indecent exposure as soon as she steps into the room. Step two: There are no other steps.

endeavors to put more men on the roof. It's an existential condition. Like a dream he had last week: all the women hated him, and the one he loved had disappeared. She started as Marcia Brady, ended up a brunette. Sharp bangs, hair the exact scent only a Czar could have the nose to imagine. More men on the roof, the Czar commands, before he retires to his quarters for the night.

THE CZAR

It has been so long since I have written.
Sometimes a little ambivalence is healthy.

The man traveled to two places: church,
and not-church. A monkey was chained

to the Formica counter of not-church.
Sometimes I find it hard to be virtuous

when wearing the corduroy slacks
of my ancestors, unresolvable as water.

I thought the red-curtain room was for
card games. I thought too deeply about

things to be counted on one hand like
the times of I dreamt of marriage to you,

something illegal in most states, the times
I studied recessive genes. Experimentation

told me we were the same thing. Was
it a coincidence: my obsession with mittens,

how you peeled them from my palms,
set them neatly atop the altar on which you

would later place me? I've lit two candles.
One for each word not written since.

The secret service wants our secret.
This is why we keep it from ourselves.

THE CZAR

Sometimes the Czar wonders if his enduring love
of Australian pop band Men at Work is ironic.

Is irony more like a casket filled with teddy bears
or a sandwich with another piece of bread inside?

Certain mornings the Czar is unsure of what he's
supposed to be doing. Compiling statistics, or

commissioning statuary. Building a waterless
fountain, or bathing in a wanderlust factory.

Solicited by the Board of Regents to define
the term "irony," the Czar hesitates and quaffs

bounteous mouthfuls of pumpkin spice latte.
Irony is a state in which every year is the New

Year. Yet this is both quite true and incorrect.
The Czar rephrases his definition: *Irony is*

an existential cure for a spiritual condition. Irony:
not to be confused with coincidence, or the Czar's

desire to fill every metaphorical hole with cement.
The Czar examines the kingdom's actuarial

tables: female life expectancy, IRA withdrawals,
wealth distribution, the jurisdiction of regret.

At night he waits in line like everybody else
at the soup kitchen. Who am I kidding? He only

thinks about waiting in line. It's the same thing,
he says to Lady Czar. The Czar dog in her lap

again. In a previous life, Lady Czar has said, the Czar
dog paced the battlefield of Gettysburg, barking

at rebels, guarding the corpses of the deceased.
Irony, the Czar thinks, *is Lady Czar in a previous life.*

THE CZAR

remembers when playmates teased him
with sticks and tickles, tied his boots

to the train tracks, claimed his name
rhymed with *benign brown pustule*.

So when all the women of Czarville
lock themselves in the fancy room

with curtains drawn, what else could
they moan? And hope a few people

might overhear? Such as husbands
and mantua makers. Playful Gladys

the milkmaid. Our Czar regrets youth
as yet another paltry sin. Playthings

do not exist in his photo booth. I
should know. I sleep there every night.

The security less than satisfactory.
No pat downs or private inspections.

My carry-on baggage riddled
with someone else's revenge fantasy.

He told me we were going to play
the Quiet Game. He told me to count

to 10 in French. It was not as difficult
as you might imagine to do both

at the same time. Even the simple tasks
involve multitasking. Like hailing

a taxi and signaling a code to your
oppressor with the same hand.

THE CZAR

wonders if his mistress is taking things
seriously. A little less time as Bjork

the swan, a little more Lady Gaga
in her meat frock. Somewhere the spin

cycle stops spinning. Somebody's ears
pop. But it's another day in this empire.

Cold feet, Advil, layers. V-neck sweaters
in the top secret paper shredder. The

Czar plans a trip to Paris but forgets
to pack the trip. His mistress suggests

what she calls the Carbonite Method.
It's a fancy name for the Czar's favorite

number, the one only he was allowed
to screen print onto his baseball jersey.

Well, he's the Czar, one parent said. We
never give up, his mistress observed,

but we might go down. She was 12, and he
was a spring training enthusiast. Now

he's a baseball card of bloated stats.
His mother never realized that Duffy's

Tee House was actually a head shop.
She inquired the price of a brilliant red

hookah, wondered where the flowers
were supposed to go, while the Czar

selected a Van Halen iron-on for front,
fuzzy Courier letters to spell out CZAR

on back (ringer tee, of course, striped
sleeves). Sometimes his mistress still

wears this shirt. It used to be her sole
garment at bedtime. Now she wears it

beneath the first of two lumberjack
flannels, practically undetectable,

much like her attachment to the Czar,
which is all undershirt, zero bra.

THE CZAR

endures the Czar of all sinus infections. He's stricken cancer from
the record, along with Lady Czar's tumultuous feet. We're all try-
ing to keep our stories as straight as a Protestant's prick, the min-
ister of the interior declares of the official narrative. But he's got
one foot in the hot tub. The other amputated years ago on the bat-
tlefield (Read: Walmart. Black Friday). And hazing's not so bad,
the Czar declares, if you can't smell the candidate's acid reflux. No
doubt his sister knows what toothpaste to smuggle into her carry-
on bag. She's all subtext, unintended consequences. Like behead-
ing a chocolate bunny on Good Friday, or the unexpected birth of a
new Czar on Michaelmas, or thereabouts. Did it surprise the gov-
erness when the Czar declared, Let me show you my sword, and he
actually whipped out a sword, his hands nowhere near his zipper?
(Read: anyone who denies Freud's omnipotence is a slug in bear
pajamas). A hippie recommended the Neti Pot, but its primitive
features sent the Czar into a rapture, reminding him of a bad foray
to Bangkok: underage he-nymph and basket suspended to the ceil-
ing. Once, in a vaporous lecture hall, a contrarian commanded the
Czar to draw upon his inner resources. Nowadays they're all
expelled into tissues and secreted inside paper cups.

THE CZAR

has been granted an honorary Doctor
of Czar Studies degree. It left him humble

not haughty. I'm joking. It left him
another donkey in a threadbare stable.

Some afternoons the Czar believes
there are too many faces in the world.

Perhaps matriculation is physical, not
emotional. Remember when your folks

dressed you as a paycheck for Halloween
and made quips about your "Virginia"?

Sometimes it feels so good to sign off
on a new piece of temporary legislation.

During sex, the Czar often spells
the word "edict" backwards, for Satan.

He smokes his pipe afterwards.
It's a disgraceful job, like logging, or

not greeting each morning with an eager
erection. The Czar prefers the Czar-

position. I would describe it or show
you a helpful photo but I'm bound

by my confidentiality agreement. The
way I like it. The Czar's Christmas list

includes the finest toes dipped
in frying oil at room temperature. Stickers

of the Czar in Technicolor covering
every nipple in sight. The Czar's bedroom,

in other words, is like the rest of the empire.
None of us here ever registered to vote.

THE CZAR

The Czar's recent lecture on the widespread panic over Asian Carp.

The Czar's cabinet: dismissed, sentenced to eternal exile, or France.

The Czar's cupboards: not enough coffee cups to contain all the
creamer.

The Czar's collection of wigs set on fire (accidentally) by Lady Czar.

The Czar's calendar on the wall of Playboy Bunnies from 1986.

The Czar's mother: not a virgin on the evening of his conception.

The Czar's mistress: too much Ecstasy, not enough caffeinated wit.

The Czar's socks always brown argyle on the first of the month.

The Czar's ties: easy to unknot after he's spiked the punch.

The Czar went down to Georgia, recalls nothing.

The Czar's obsession: Juliette Binoche, or other brunettes, circa 1996.

The Czar's preferred currency precludes a background check.

The Czar's undergarments always thrown out with the newspaper.

The Czar's owl perched atop the bronze statue of the Czar.

The Czar's regrets: erased from his hard drive, ripped onto yours.

The Czar's orgasm sometimes referred to as the Blue Screen of Death.

The Czar's teachers always corrected his grammar, adjusted his posture.

The Czar's teachers in college always said he earned his grades.

The Czar's virginity: given to a bag checker like a souvenir.

The Czar's definition of *vagina dentata*: paper shredder + sublimation.

The Czar tried out for the role of Swedenborgian mystic in the play.

The Czar is always responsible for "No Woman No Cry" on the jukebox.

The Czar's favorite cash crop: the kind for whipping horse flanks.

The Czar pictured in front of an extinct typewriter, confused.

The Czar trembles while explicating "The Flea," since it's about him.

The Czar left Chicago and (kind of) never looked back.

THE CZAR

Some people long for an imaginary twin.

That feeling of dropping a book to the floor
and having it caught by your gorgeous double

and it's not a dream, it's a story you're reading

before you drop the book to the unsavory
hardwood, a sentimental rag rug beneath

the bed, which is actually for two, or nearly

two, a kind of mathematics the Czar employs
when "cutting the fat," or managing passions

with the stealth of a savvy upper administrator.

Some people long for the unspeakable. The
Czar desires everything, talks to himself, but

he's really calling the invisible, like passing

the gravy to yourself. It's still your mother's
secret recipe and servants with rubber gloves,

a place setting for a guest likely not to come,

like the Czar's dignitaries of German origins:
ripe with innuendo and the Theory of Relativity.

THE CZAR

Someone sends me a text message
announcing his "new phone number."

I reply with a photograph of burned
acorn squash, claim it's the part

surgeons took out all those years
back, and does it look at all familiar?

The Czar's missives are delivered
but never sent. His God four-person'd.

His geese manufacturing their own
foie gras. The distant freight train

unpacks itself down to bedroom size,
making a makeshift table out of

the orgy of our tangled legs. The Czar
is not on Twitter. He owns Twitter.

Like how sometimes you wake up
and the morning coffee has been made

already. The Czar is the first thing
on the Czar's list of things to do, and

everyone else's. What comes next is
predictable: execution, expansion,

trips to the dollar store for dryer sheets.
The Czar's automobiles produce

their own foreign oil. He has thought
about driving the car. Sometimes

this is enough. Sometimes he commands
the Mercedes parked in leaves, lets

the catalytic converter vocalize its own
fantasies. There is no Czar but Czar,

his mother whispered when she spoke
of his father prior to the revolt.

THE CZAR

overestimates interest in his speaking tour.
Nobody wants to pay for a private box
in the athenaeum. He rushes, but he's not

Rush. He once shared a toilet with _____
_____. Tell no one, but the Czar
has been charged with public intercourse

ever since the first time he tried it (alone).
The police bought his specious claim
of private sphere reassignment syndrome.

At home, Lady Czar builds an anatomically-
correct effigy of a rival Czar,
transforms it into a neutered commoner.

The Czar loses numerous sizeable deposits
in the local park, then has to fork
over funds to hire stadium seat-warmers

at fifty a pop, minus the pop. His approval
rating droops, like the many-colored
pants of the jester every June at the festival

of lights. It isn't a festival, really, and there
aren't any lights. The joke's on us,
Lady Czar says to the effigy of her rival.

She stares at her breasts like the royal dog
turning his head at high-pitched sounds.
When the Czar dresses as the perfect non-Czar,

complete with a flannel shirt, mustard stains
in his fake beard, he slips off to the park
again. Everybody knows what comes next.

THE CZAR

Every road was Snow Road.
>Every man was Czar.

Every woman was a bank
>of snow worth falling into

at least three times.
>Every day was throwback

Thursday, because my
>back was a sort of map.

Don't believe me? Look.
>The Czar deleted my entire

electromagnetic field.
>It used to be a wheat field.

I'd pound my palms against
>something vaguely

artisanal, hoping for a week
>of Tuesdays. Every article

of clothing ended up on
>the wrong floor, or stuck

on a mannequin's excuse
>for skin. Don't believe me?

The newspaper had a full
      page ad to prove it back

when we had newspapers and
      meaningful telephone poles.

The ink never left my fingers.
      So what if I dreamt nightly

of transference? Every
      pill prescribed to me by

the Czar hadn't been tested
      on the peasant children.

Every presence was not
      an absence. Clearly

they'd rigged another
      election, served hors d'oeuvres.

Nothing left but a stack
      of toothpicks on a platter.

THE CZAR

claims he's losing his selective hearing. He's drowning, and Lady Czar floats away the afternoon on a pink inflatable cushion in the royal pool. His mistress formulates a game plan for the Mall of America. From where the Czar sits, the water looks green. When the birds start bitching, the Czar hears all the sirens he banished to a hippie collective in Wyoming. He's a massage without a happy ending, his mistress says. As always, she's buried beneath a pile of fuck-me pumps. As if life was one more round of Pin the Needle on My Nipple. But he can't even hear her muffled sounds. She's a choker away from a bad habit. A gateway drug. It's better this way, says one limb to its dysfunctional other. Once, the Czar's mother was not the Czar's mother. She was June, and her hair was so long people used it to truss chickens. She would call out the rear casement to her boys, but nary a head would turn until the milkmaids passed with their whorish regalia and clattering buckets. Some people, like me, can feel the presence of another person in the room. The opposite is also true. Perhaps it's most accurate to say that while I feel your absence, I never sense the absence of the Czar. Once there was a field filled with the most ridiculous jackdaws. But it wasn't here.

THE CZAR

is a silly old thing. He believes
Prairie Lights is an organic cigarette.

So when a slacker from his
Academic Success Seminar offers

a hacky sack and a beanie,
the Czar spouts something about

hipster Millennials, reasons
for still boiling water in a country

where the taps are uber
clean. The Czar thinks Pooh Bear

is a bathhouse he accidentally
intruded upon in Vancouver, back

in his heavy immigrant days.
The Czar never looked up the word

neologism, but now figures
it's a third variety of female orgasm,

a newfound one. For years
this particular Czar rode the flaky

coattails of throwback chic:
<< I am a throwback >> he said

in his native tongue, dance
floor holding back dry heaves due

to the spiked jukebox spitting
out the Beach Boys B-side collection.

Sometimes the Czar claims his
pants feel like fish scales. Other times

he's not wearing any pants. He
can smell the implants on a stripper's

breath, stares at fruit baskets
like they're French quotation marks.

THE CZAR

has not finished all of his holiday shopping.
This should not surprise you. You passed

a rigorous background check to gain
access to this private information. Credit

card numbers and penis dimensions not
included. That's for the premiere club.

Anyway, the Czar has purchased nothing
for you, nor for me, because he does not

know we're on to him. Perhaps it's time
for me to share the fact that we are sole

spectators to this spectacle. We put mono
in this particular monocle. Except there's

two of us. Trifles. Let's say a man sits down
in a room across from you, and that man

is me. I'm going to wrestle your pants off
someday, and you're going to call in sick

from work but not because you're sick
is what my eyes telepathically suggest,

and you might say we're both AM radios
that appreciate this frequency, even if we

desire to seduce the cliché morning FM
deejay at the same time. I put a red bow

around your vulnerable neck, and then I
gave you my long underwear at 50% off,

though the sale promised to continue on
long after midnight. I can't promise you

12 days of Christmas, just the privilege
of shepherding our Czar to fruition.

THE CZAR

cries sometimes when he listens to the Gregg Allman band.
Don't judge, okay? It's much better than sobbing through

the national anthem, especially considering that the Czar's
national anthem includes the following images and phrases:

The velvet shudder of your concrete curtain . . .

Like three alligators fighting over one untuned violin . . .

The next morning I donned my fur hat and fled again . . .

Sonja rolled her stockings like venison powder into a gun . . .

Oh _____! *Oh* _____! Was that the sea, my lost one, or the gin . . .

You wrote your name in all my books, same green pen . . .

Huffy Czar hid the day. Unappeasable the Czar slept in . . .

So many ripped stockings, so many bald intentions . . .

Two teenagers playing nicely with each other in a playpen . . .

Three ice cubes, melting into the shape of our sins. . . .

Sonja on the phone. She speaks fluently in Ritalin . . .

The Czar, his mistress dressed up as Emperor Penguins . . .

Lingerie as bookmarks, other postmodern inventions . . .

Copies of *Wuthering Heights* in the man cave and the den...

The lyrics to hair metal ballads translated in French...

Lady Czar saluting her whorehouse of diamonds...

The bombs bursting in air and all over her chin...

Like your shoulder against my shoulder again and again...

A placid genius, sometimes I aspire to recreate your skin...

Unlike other youth of his age, the Czar seldom fancied
a stroll on the moor in his nightclothes, preferred dogs

to be sincere in their hostilities, and never saluted while
his country's flag was wheeled away on a golden stretcher.

THE CZAR

attends a symposium on Wordles. The parts and pieces in all their
right part places. The Hilton recast as The Grand Tax Ballroom
Exclusive. The Czar parks his horse at a meter. It's a weekend for
turning tropes into trophy wives, renaming his favorite football
team the 69ers. In the hotel lobby it's man on man on woman cov-
erage. Hot reads at the bar. Then he blitzes into the bathroom with
a Swedish flight attendant to hide the meatballs. Everybody's
briefcases playing footsie underneath the table in their absence.
When it's time to head home, though, he checks out another room.
Wordles cover the walls, a stranger in the bathroom with the low-
rise jeans to prove it. The perfect holiday recipe for success: dis-
traction. Apparently the Czar is using too many words and all of
them all too often. But it's hard to diversify your vocabulary when
you're not giving Java permission to run on your laptop. Your lap-
top is an altar, after all. The Czar remembers nuns and their dia-
tribes against preposition pile-up. So when he piles himself up a
new receptionist, it's not just the phones that are being answered
promptly. It's like the Operation game without a body, or a scalpel.
It's like Nabokov without the shuddering. It's like a poster session
where every poster is deliciously blank.

THE CZAR

has never been anyone's "little favorite."
Not even the nursemaid hired to raise him.

His father was mostly a corporate sponsor.
Aunts wrapped the Czar's pedigree in wax

and fed him unremarkable porridge. Yet
there were no true old country hardships.

Not even an unpleasant legacy to exploit
without effort. When pursued, the Czar

had nothing to tell his crusty biographer.
His life was one sheep shy of amazing.

*

The Czar has been someone's "little favorite."
Particularly the nursemaid hired to raise him.

His father wasn't the first Czar after all.
Just another Kevin in a long line of Kevins.

The nursemaid made pasta from scratch,
long noodles like lederhosen. The Czar

refused all other formative experiences,
sucked cough drops. Even then his private

thoughts weren't private. The nursemaid
a take-home test. No Czar Left Behind.

*

Favorites don't last forever. They're not
even multi-orgasmic, and certainly not

multi-step equations. Yet you may find
yourself a bit of an historical revisionist.

Par example: I'm never giving this film
back to Netflix. I find myself sneaking

scenes between appointments, like hand
sanitizer blasts, or screams into the trash.

Why didn't we ever watch movies together?
Oh, yes. Because you are the Czar. Right.

*

Forever is a long time, his mistress says.
She scans the New Releases at Family

Video. The Czar offers an easy joke about
his most recent orgasm. The paparazzi

fight over the right angle to photograph
Lady Czar's bikini. Red as a poinsettia.

Her breasts blush. At least she wears one
of those fur hats. It's mid-winter. What's

she thinking? one squirrel says to the other,
fighting over old linguini in the alley.

THE CZAR

seldom notices he's stressed until he's stressed
beyond repair. He's an import, remember.

A more exotic carburetor means fewer bucks
left over and secondhand cookies for all

but the finest love children. The Czar cut his
teeth on ball bearings and other hazards

such as Zwieback and Schadenfreude Crisp.
What, you haven't tried it? Blame lack

of an authentic _____-an grandmother.
Blame the silly stand of trees over there.

Your mother put you in a pram then pushed
and ran. Your first steps were a fall.

The Czar's mother hired two nannies. One
for the Czar; one for herself. The rumors

about the affair between both nannies and
the Czar's mother was mostly based on

who did whose dirty laundry and hung it
on the branch of an oak tree outside

the Czar's bedroom window. This caused
the Czar consternation. His therapist

prescribed three hours of morning television
every afternoon and endless games

of Risk. Once, the Czar ate Luxembourg
for a snack. All the thimbles revolted.

Monopoly never recovered. It's difficult
to play two board games at the same

time. Especially if you rule the whole world.
But the Czar learned it from his mother.

THE CZAR

has a list of regrets. It's short, and ghost-written.

Sometimes other people enjoy works of literature
and close the cover then drink a fine glass of water.

The Czar is fully aware he'll never be his own ghost

because that would require, you know, some longing.
He's a full set of parentheses, a packed gold locket.

Eternal virginity, in a way, because nothing tears him.

He wonders about all the rooms he ever slept in, not
out of sentiment, but maybe he left a favorite hat.

Maybe cobwebs made a daguerreotype of his visage.

Or perhaps a pair of yoga pants will come along, be
his eternal savior. The Czar's sister has dimples, but

not in her cheeks. Her shoulders. Maybe this explains

his overuse of the exclamation point and air quotes,
which he considers foreplay. The necessary regrets

congregate. Like quitting book club before book club

quits you. Save the Date anyway, the Czar's sister said,
holding a stick that once held a red velvet cakesicle.

Somebody gets the last laugh. Somebody gets crumbs.

ACKNOWLEDGMENTS

To the organizations we have been conscripted into and/or overthrown, we offer our sincere thanks: the state of Ohio, the republic of Michigan, the University of Akron, Ashland University, the Big Big Mess reading series, the University of Akron Press, and *Barn Owl Review.*

To the kingdom of Black Lawrence Press and its many noble dignitaries, including Diane Goettel, Gina Keicher, Kit Frick, and designer Amy Freels: we doff our caps again and again and again.

To our families, both acknowledged and unacknowledged: thank you eternally for your support.

To Elizabeth Colen, Matthew Guenette, and Carol Guess: we salute you for your friendship and the kind words emblazoned upon this heady tome. Please join us for a parlor game at your earliest convenience.

To our mothers who taught us to read and created the Czar within us in various sitting rooms and on chaise lounges and/or fainting couches metaphorical and literal.

To mentors and teachers who supported, guided, upbraided, and knew not what they Czarred and therefore shall always be forgiven.

To the kind beasts who inhabit and inhabited our kingdom. May they always have prime real estate in the lap of the Czar.

To the Czar himself: long may he reign. There is no Czar but Czar, and his court is filled with many Czars, one nesting into the next until dancing atop a pin, a Czar smaller than human eye can see, yet legion nonetheless.

Mary Biddinger is the author of four full-length collections of poetry, most recently *Small Enterprise* (Black Lawrence Press, 2015). She is Professor of English at the University of Akron, where she teaches poetry writing and literature, and edits the Akron Series in Poetry at the University of Akron Press. Biddinger is the recipient of a 2015 National Endowment for the Arts creative writing fellowship in poetry, and is currently working on a book-length volume of prose poems.

Jay Robinson teaches at Ashland University and The University of Akron. He's also the Co-Editor-in-Chief/Reviews Editor for *Barn Owl Review* and helps edit The Akron Series in Contemporary Poetics. Poetry and prose has appeared in *32 Poems*, *The Laurel Review*, *Poetry*, *Whiskey Island*, among others. *The Czar* is his first book.